This Girl
- A diary just for girls -

CREATED BY:

Elle Simms

A MINDFULNESS JOURNAL FOR KIDS FILLED WITH WRITING PROMPTS,
INSPIRATIONAL QUOTES, THINGS TO DRAW AND COLOR AND MUCH MORE.

FIND MORE AWESOME KIDS' BOOKS AT

www.ellesimms.com

Boring Legal Stuff

Instructions

Fill every inch of this book with words, pictures, and color.
Express yourself. Be bold and daring!

And remember...

THIS JOURNAL is about THIS GIRL

and nobody else.

Embrace the things that make you unique and stand out in this world.

*"No one ever made a difference by being
like everyone else."* ~ P. T. Barnum

Fill in this book with meraki.

meraki

(V.) TO DO SOMETHING WITH SOUL, CREATIVITY,
OR LOVE; TO PUT SOMETHING OF YOURSELF IN YOUR WORK.

*If you use markers, please use the pages at the
back of this book to test for bleed-through.*

This girl's name is:

all

about

me

At This Moment

 Where I am right now:

 The kind of day it is:

 The song in my head:

 The book I am reading:

 Last movie I watched:

 Last thing I ate:

 How I feel right now:

 The last person I talked to was:

 I wish…

My First Memory

THE

B E S T

song:

show:

food:

actor:

candy:

smell:

game:

place:

book:

&

THE

W O R S T

song:

show:

food:

actor:

candy:

smell:

game:

place:

book:

These are
a few
favo

of my rite things!

What I am
E-X-C-I-T-E-D
About

A LITTLE KNOWN FACT ABOUT ME IS...

SOMETHING I WISH EVERYONE KNEW ABOUT ME IS...

IF I COULD WRITE A BOOK IT WOULD BE ABOUT...

THE BEST PART OF THE DAY IS USUALLY...

SHOOT FOR THE
moon

ALL THE THINGS
THAT I'M GOOD AT

AWARDS I HAVE WON

EVEN IF YOU MISS
YOU'LL LAND AMONG THE
stars

The last time I tried something new was:

Something I have always wanted to try is:

My Favorite Book

My Kind
of Music

All-Time Favorites Playlist

WHAT I THINK ABOUT LOVE

how to
be a
better
me

Do not try to be better
than everyone else. Try to
be better than the person
you were yesterday.

THIS IS ME

Create a self-portrait.

What I like most about myself is...

THESE ARE
~ *my* ~
# VALUES

values
(N.) A PERSON'S
PRINCIPLES OR
STANDARDS OF BEHAVIOR;
ONE'S JUDGMENT OF
WHAT IS IMPORTANT
IN LIFE

WAYS THAT
I CAN REMAIN TRUE
TO MY VALUES:

integrity

DOING THE RIGHT THING, EVEN WHEN NO ONE IS WATCHING

Ways I can be a better person:

It is not about having the best of everything. It is about giving the best of yourself.

I am grateful for...

Times that someone showed me
KINDNESS

Times I have been kind to others:

THINGS

I want to achieve:

Write about a challenge you
faced and what you learned from it.

Something I struggle with is...

This is my plan to overcome it:

PRETEND YOU HAVE A DAUGHTER YOUR AGE.

Write a letter of advice to her.

the world around me

ADVENTURE
is out there

PLACES I HAVE TRAVELED:

PLACES I WOULD LOVE TO VISIT:

wanderlust
(N.) A STRONG DESIRE OR
URGE TO TRAVEL AND
EXPLORE THE WORLD

The place I live...

Where I live:

The best thing about it:

The worst thing about it:

If I could live anywhere in the world I would choose:

What my home is like:

My Dream House

I can make the world a better place by...

The place I hang out with my friends:

The place I go when I'm lonely or sad:

My favorite place at school:

Where I usually spend my summer vacation:

words

are

powerful

Fill these two
pages with
positive words
and messages
to yourself.

Something someone once told me that made me feel really good:

Words someone once said that changed my opinion about something:

Make someone feel good.

COLOR IN A CIRCLE EVERY TIME YOU
SAY SOMETHING NICE TO SOMEONE.

Write a Poem

The funniest thing I ever heard:

The best advice I was ever given:

A time when my words were very powerful:

Something I read that moved me was:

One Word...

Pick one word and write it over and over
in all different styles and colors.

dream
BIG

IF YOUR DREAMS DON'T SCARE YOU THEY'RE JUST NOT BIG ENOUGH.

The biggest dream I have is...

Bucket

All the things
i want to do
before i die

List

IF I HAD SUPERPOWERS

My dream job is...

If I had a million dollars I would...

A dream that became reality:

Current Wish List

goals & plans

A GOAL IS A DREAM WITH A PLAN AND A DEADLINE.

How is your life different than it was a year ago?

Can you think of something you quit doing that you wish you hadn't?

What is something you wish you had spent more time doing two years ago, that would make a difference in your life today?

What is your biggest accomplishment?

Take something from your wish list and turn it into a goal.

Goal:

Plan:

What I want to be doing...

In 2 years:

In 5 years:

When I am an adult:

Myself at 80 Years Old

Draw a picture. What have you accomplished?

When you are 80 what will matter most to you?

If nothing ever changed there would be no *butterflies*

Ready for a Change!

A BAD HABIT I AM GOING TO BREAK:

A NEW HABIT I WILL FORM:

A NEW SKILL I AM GOING TO LEARN:

A BOOK I WILL READ:

A NEW FOOD I WILL TRY:

this

girl's

emotions

I AM...

What would make you happy right now?

What do you need more of in your life?

What are you scared of?

How can you overcome your fear?

Dear Me

I love you because…

Things I am proud of:

The things I think but cannot say:

The scariest thing I have ever done:

What I would do differently if I knew nobody would judge me:

Write down
a prayer

the people in my life

My Family

DRAW / TELL ABOUT YOUR FAMILY.

My Pets

If you do not have any, then the ones you wish you had

My Friends

Things I like to do with my friends and family:

Someone who I would like to reconnect with:

Someone who inspires me and why:

The person who has impacted my life the most and how:

A PERSON I AM ANGRY WITH:

HOW I CAN FORGIVE THEM:

forgiveness
IS GOOD FOR THE SOUL BECAUSE
STAYING ANGRY ROBS US OF HAPPINESS

If I could spend the day with anybody...

Alive, dead, real or fictional - anyone!

feelin'

good

HAPPINESS

is enjoying the little things in life

ALLTHE THINGS THAT MAKE ME

happy

My Favorite Jokes

The Perfect Day

WHAT WOULD IT BE LIKE?

something
beautiful

Find something beautiful. Examine it.
Draw a picure or take a photograph of it.
explain why you find it beautiful.

Things that give me comfort

List ways to create beauty around you.

My Proudest Moment

Small Victories

Write down the times when things go just right for you.

Stuff to Remember

More Stuff to Remember

Books to Read

Movies to Watch

Savings Tracker

How much money can you save?
Color in the jar as you add to your savings
until it is full and see how much you saved.

- $
- $
- $
- $
- $
- $
- $
- $
- $
- $
- $
- $

Notes

Notes

Notes

Notes

Notes

Notes

FOR MORE GREAT BOOKS VISIT

www.ellesimms.com

If you enjoyed this book
please leave a review on

www.amazon.com

Thanky you!